# AVOCA
# Salads

# Contents

# Introduction

Salads to start, salads to accompany, salads for lunch, for picnics and big celebrations – there really is no end of occasions when these simple assemblies lift a table. It's something to do with the colour. But also the texture and shape. Healthy too. Think of different leaves, of other vegetables, flowers and fruit. Peaches in a green salad on a hot summer day, or walnuts in the autumn.

Freshness of ingredients is paramount in a salad; you need colour and vibrancy, so buy frequently, locally and seasonally and organic if possible. Farmers' markets and independent greengrocers tend to be better hunting grounds than supermarkets. Most ingredients can be stored in the fridge for a day. Herbs and leaves for example, need to be wrapped loosely in plastic bags and stored at the bottom of the fridge.

Contrast is important in a good salad. Variety of both colour and texture provide interest; succulent redness of roasted peppers with bitter leaves, or fiery, crunchy radishes sliced wafer thin to show off their creamy white interior. At Avoca we like to add extras; nuts and seeds as well as lots of herbs. We use up to 10 kilos of herbs a day in the cafés. That's a lot of picking and chopping but we feel herbs are crucial.

At Avoca we make a lot of salads using potatoes, pulses and grains. They are full of flavour and have fantastic textures and colours. It is important to dress pulses while they are still hot. That way they absorb the flavours of the dressing and more robust ingredients. Leave the herbs until last, when everything is cool, otherwise they will wilt and turn brown.

We also use cheese quite a lot. It brings richness, but also a tangy saltiness – think crumbled feta, goat's cheese and blue cheese. Scattered over some well-dressed leaves and eaten with bread this quickly becomes lunch, or a substantial snack at least.

When to serve salads if they are part of a larger meal can be something of a dilemma. Some feel it's a nice clean way to finish things off. The Americans tend to have them as first courses and there is no doubt the colour and vibrancy is quite a scene setter. The wonderful thing about salads is that they are so versatile. Try and see which way works best for you.

***All recipes feed four unless otherwise stated.***

# Minted petit pois and Swiss chard with lardons

*extra virgin olive oil*
*6 slices streaky bacon or pancetta, cut into lardons*
*200g frozen petits pois*
*1 garlic clove, peeled and crushed with a little salt*
*1 bunch mint, finely chopped*
*1 small red onion, peeled and thinly sliced*
*200g baby Swiss chard or baby spinach*
*juice of 1 lemon*
*50g feta cheese, crumbled*

Heat a dessertpoon of olive oil in a frying pan and cook the bacon lardons over a moderate heat for 3-4 minutes, or until they start to crisp up.

Defrost (you can plunge the unopened bag into warm water for 30 minutes) the petits pois and mix with the garlic, mint, red onion and chard.

Dress with the garlic, mint, red onion, spinach and 4 tablespoons olive oil, and season with salt, pepper and lemon juice to taste. Add in the bacon and sprinkle the feta on top.

. . . . . . . . . . . . . . . . . . . . . . . . . . . . . . . . . . . . . . . . . . . . . . . . .

*Tip*
*Season sparingly as both the bacon and feta tend to be quite salty.*

The lemon juice will turn the peas yellow after about an hour so add just before serving.

# Tabbouleh

*100g burghul wheat*
*juice of 2 lemons*
*4-5 tablespoons extra*
*virgin olive oil*
*3 generous bunches parsley*
*(about 250g), finely chopped*
*1 large bunch mint (about*
*70g without stems), roughly*
*chopped*
*1 bunch scallions, trimmed*
*and finely sliced*
*1 cucumber, trimmed,*
*seeded and diced*
*4 tomatoes, cored and*
*roughly chopped*

*The success of this salad lies in using lots and lots of herbs. It may seem extravagant, but it is the herbs that really make it work. Burghul is a wheat that has been boiled, dried and then ground. It is like a denser couscous.*

Soak the burghul in plenty of cold water for an hour, drain and squeeze. Combine with the lemon juice and season with salt and pepper. Stir and set aside for 10 minutes. It will start to absorb the lemon juice and swell.

Add the oil and stir again. Add the remaining ingredients, except the tomatoes. Stir well, check the seasoning and set aside in the fridge until ready to serve.

Spread out on a large plate, scatter over the tomatoes and serve.

## Tips

*This is great served on its own with little gem lettuce leaves used to scoop it up. Alternatively, serve with grilled meat or fish, along with some salsa.*

*It keeps particularly well, and is almost better the next day when the flavours have been allowed to get to know one another.*

*This is a good example of where it really pays to use extra virgin olive oil. The flavour is altogether bigger and fruitier, with loads of character.*

# Spiced potato and bean with roast red peppers

3 red peppers, seeded and cut into thick strips
8 tablespoons olive oil
450g new potatoes, washed and halved
2 teaspoons powdered Cajun spice
1 x 400g can black kidney beans, rinsed and well drained
1 x 400g can cannellini beans, rinsed and well drained
1 bunch scallions, finely sliced
2 garlic cloves, peeled and finely chopped
2 chillies, finely chopped
1 bunch flat-leaf parsley, finely chopped

*Easy to prepare ahead of time, this is a salad to have on its own or with barbecued meat or fish.*

Preheat the oven to 180C/gas mark 4.

Toss the red pepper strips in 2 tablespoons olive oil and roast for 10-15 minutes, turning occasionally. Transfer the peppers to a bowl and cover with clingfilm. When cool enough to handle peel.

Toss the potatoes in the Cajun spice and remaining olive oil, season with salt and pepper, and roast for 30-40 minutes or until tender. You need to toss the potatoes once or twice during this time.

When the potatoes are cooked, combine with the beans, scallions, garlic, chilli and roasted peppers. Toss so everything is well coated. Allow to cool and add the parsley, salt and pepper and toss again.

*Garden parsley*

# Fig, goat's cheese and
# pine nuts

4 handfuls mixed rocket, red
chard and baby spinach
4 tablespoons olive oil
1 teaspoon balsamic vinegar
200g soft goat's curd
4 figs
1 tablespoon pine nuts

*This salad is best made towards the end of the summer and into the autumn when figs are at their best. Look out for fruit that is well perfumed, soft and just a little giving.*

Season the salad leaves with salt and pepper and toss with the olive oil and balsamic. Pile on to 4 plates, or on to a serving plate.

Break up the goat's curd and scatter over the leaves. Quarter the figs and arrange on top.

Toast the pine nuts lightly in a hot dry frying pan until just coloured. Watch them carefully as they burn very easily. Allow to cool slightly. Scatter over the salad and serve.

## Variations
*You could add blanched French beans, or use feta or mozzarella cheese instead of the goat's cheese.*

## Tips
*We use Boile, but other soft goat's cheese can be used.*

*Spices*

It is far better to buy spices whole, toast them in a dry frying pan over a moderate heat and then grind them as you use them. Pre-ground spices oxidise and lose their freshness and aroma more quickly than whole ones. When buying, wholefood stores tend to have better quality and are more economic than supermarkets.

Dried

*pastas and pulses to keep*

*in stock include:*

Couscous

Bulghur wheat

Barley

Chickpeas

Red and black kidney

beans

Flageolet beans

Cannellini beans

*Dried pasta*

*& pulses*

# *Food in cans and jars*

**I**talian brands of pulses are usually excellent and a much better way of sourcing for smaller numbers. In the cafés we would cook all pulses from scratch, but then we are dealing with somewhat larger volumes! Just make sure to rinse them well under plenty of cold water.

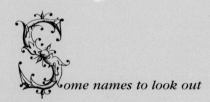

**S**ome names to look out *for on cans:*

John West smoked tuna fillet in oil.

Ortiz tuna in oil.

Ortiz asparagus stalks – (stock up that suitcase when you are next on holiday).

Ortiz anchovy fillets in olive oil. (Ortiz is an excellent brand but there are Italian and Spanish brands, often in jars, which are also good.)

Suma organic chickpeas are very good.

Italian brands generally offer superior eating.

# Roast red pepper and chickpeas

*3 red peppers, cut into thick strips*
*6 tablespoons olive oil*
*2 x 400g cans chickpeas, rinsed and drained*
*2 garlic cloves, peeled and finely chopped*
*2 teaspoons ground cumin*
*1 teaspoon ground coriander*
*juice of 1 lemon*
*1 bunch flat-leaf parsley, finely chopped*
*1 bunch scallions, finely chopped*

Preheat the oven to 180C/gas mark 4. Toss the red pepper strips in 2 tablespoons olive oil and roast for 10-15 minutes, turning occasionally. Transfer the peppers to a bowl and cover with clingfilm. When cool enough to handle peel.

Heat the remaining olive oil in a saucepan and add the chickpeas. Toss in the oil and heat through for 5 minutes. Add the garlic and spices and cook for a further 2-3 minutes or until the spices start to lose their raw aroma. Season with salt and pepper as you go, and taste.

Transfer the chickpeas to a bowl, add the pepper strips and season with lemon juice. Add the parsley and scallions and toss.

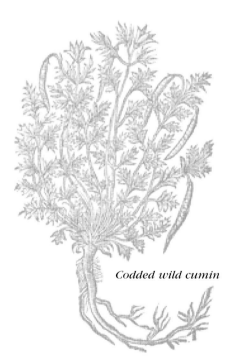

***Codded wild cumin***

# Oriental bean sprout
## and egg noodle

5 tablespoons sesame oil
3 garlic cloves, peeled and
finely chopped
2cm piece of fresh ginger,
peeled and finely chopped
6 tablespoons soy sauce
40g egg thread noodles
1 yellow and 2 red peppers,
cut into strips
110g mangetout, blanched,
refreshed and cut into strips,
or 110g broccoli florets,
blanched and refreshed
A bunch of spring onions,
trimmed and sliced
at an angle
700g bean sprouts

*A taste of Asia, but nothing too dramatic. What little heat there is comes from the ginger so no chilli kick. The idea of cold noodles as a salad is surprisingly refreshing on a hot summer's day.*

Gently heat the sesame oil in a frying pan, taking care not to let it burn; this can easily happen, as sesame oil burns at quite a low temperature. Add the garlic and ginger and sauté gently for 2 minutes or until lightly golden. Stir in the soy sauce and allow to cool.
Cook the egg noodles according to the instructions on the packet. Drain well, add them to the sesame oil and soy mixture and leave to cool. Mix all the vegetables and the bean sprouts with the cooled noodles, along with any of the optional additions.

## Optional additions
*Roasted peanuts, water chestnuts, diced cooked chicken breast, cooked prawns.*

# Mushroom, French bean and bacon

350g button mushrooms, quartered
4 tablespoons olive oil
juice of 1 lemon
a large handful of French beans, trimmed
1/2 teaspoon harissa
1 tablespoon Avoca semi-sun-dried tomato pesto
1 red chilli, finely chopped
2 garlic cloves, peeled and finely chopped
1 bunch parsley, finely chopped
1 tablespoon flaked almonds

*A classic combination but all the better for that. You can vary the mushrooms, adding in wild varieties like porcini and morels, depending on season and budget*

Sauté the mushrooms in the olive oil for 5 minutes or until just starting to wilt. Season with salt and pepper. You may need to do this in batches. Toss in lemon juice to prevent discoloration.

Blanch the beans in well-salted boiling water, refresh briefly in cold water, then drain and toss with the harissa, sun-dried tomato pesto, chilli and garlic while still warm. Add the mushrooms to this mixture and stir in the parsley.

Lightly toast the almonds in a dry frying pan until just coloured and scatter over the salad. Check the seasoning and serve.

## Variation
*Dried porcini, reconstituted in warm water and mixed with field or button mushrooms, produce a slightly stronger flavour.*

Mushrooms:

For their size button mushrooms punch way above their weight. A kind of king of the cultivated world. There they sit all small and closed. Yet fried in a little oil or butter they reveal autumnal, forest notes. Sliced raw and tossed into a salad they bring subtlety.

# New potato, pea and dill

*200g fresh or frozen peas*
*12 small new potatoes, cleaned*
*and cut into 1cm slices*
*2 eggs*
*4 tablespoons extra virgin*
*olive oil*
*1 tablespoon soured cream*
*2 scallions, trimmed and*
*finely chopped*
*4 tablespoons finely*
*chopped dill*
*2 lemons, halved*

Cook the peas in unsalted boiling water (salt toughens the skins) for barely 2 minutes if frozen, about 5 if fresh. Remove and refresh under cold water. Add the potatoes to the boiling water, which should now be salted. Cook for 8-10 minutes, or until tender and remove. Boil the eggs for 8 minutes, remove, refresh under cold water, peel, halve and roughly chop.

Scatter the potatoes and peas over 4 plates. Whisk the olive oil into the soured cream, season with salt and pepper and thin with a little warm water. Drizzle this over the potatoes, then sprinkle over the scallions, chopped dill and chopped egg. Season all with salt and pepper, and serve with a lemon half on the side.

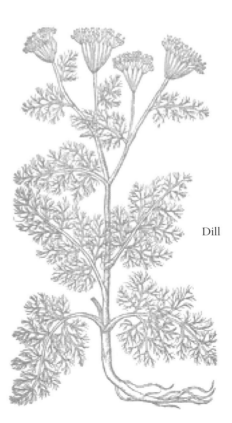

Dill

# Ploughman's lunch

*1 celery heart, diced*
*1 Granny Smith apple, cored, diced and tossed in a little lemon juice*
*1 red apple, cored, diced and tossed in a little lemon juice*
*1 small red onion, peeled and finely diced*
*1 bunch parsley, finely chopped*
*4 tablespoons Kilmacanogue French dressing (see page 22)*
*hunk good-quality Cheddar, cut into cubes*

*An ideal autumn salad when the apples start to come in. Vary by using different cheeses.*

Combine everything but the cheese in a bowl and toss well, seasoning with salt and pepper.

Sprinkle over the cheese and serve.

*A salad*

*is about*

*many things,*

*but not*

*too many,*

*or confusion*

*results*

# Beans and barley

200g pearl barley
500ml vegetable stock
4 tablespoons olive oil
2 garlic cloves, peeled and
finely sliced
a pinch of dried chilli flakes
1 x 400g can red kidney
beans, rinsed and drained
1 x 400g can black kidney
beans, rinsed and drained
100g frozen petits pois,
thawed (there is no need
to cook them)
1 bunch coriander,
roughly chopped
1 bunch flat-leaf parsley,
leaves picked
1 bunch scallions,
finely chopped
a handful of mangetout,
briefly blanched in salted
water and refreshed in
cold water
4 tablespoons semi-sun-dried
tomatoes
1 tablespoon white
wine vinegar

*This is a really healthy salad. The combination of pulses and grains forms a sort of vegetarian dietary nirvana, which means energy is released slowly over the following few hours.*

Rinse the barley in plenty of cold water, cover with vegetable stock in a saucepan, bring to the boil and simmer until tender, about 30 minutes. Strain.

Heat the olive oil in a saucepan and gently sauté the garlic and chilli until the garlic just starts to colour. Remove from the heat and add the strained beans, peas and barley and toss so everything is well coated. Cover and heat through for a couple of minutes so everything is warmed through.

Add the herbs, scallions, mangetout and sun-dried tomatoes, season with salt and pepper and vinegar and toss so everything is well mixed.

*dressings*

# Avoca French dressing

Makes 800ml

*200ml red or white wine vinegar*
*200ml extra virgin olive oil*
*400ml sunflower oil*
*1 garlic clove, peeled and finely chopped*
*3 tablespoons wholegrain mustard*
*1-2 tablespoons honey, depending on preference*

Blend in a processor and season with salt and pepper to taste. This will keep for a couple of weeks in the fridge.

# Caesar dressing

Makes 500ml

*8 anchovy fillets, mashed*
*3 garlic cloves, peeled and finely chopped*
*5 medium egg yolks*
*500ml sunflower oil*
*125g Parmesan, freshly grated*
*5 drops Worcestershire sauce*

Whisk the anchovy fillets and garlic into the egg yolks. Gradually add the sunflower oil, drop by drop, until you form an emulsion. Then add in a steady stream. Whisk in the Parmesan and Worcestershire sauce, check seasoning and serve.

## N.B.
You need to use dark anchovy fillets not the cured white ones which will not mash.

# Suffolk Street balsamic dressing

Makes 600ml

*150ml balsamic vinegar*
*300ml extra virgin olive oil*
*150ml walnut or hazelnut oil*
*1 tablespoon Dijon mustard*
*1 garlic clove, peeled and finely chopped*

Blend in a processor and season with salt and pepper to taste. This will keep for a couple of weeks in the fridge.

# Mayonnaise

Makes 500ml

500ml sunflower oil
5 medium egg yolks
½ teaspoon Dijon mustard
juice of 1 lemon

Whisk the sunflower oil, drop by drop, into the egg yolks and mustard until you form an emulsion. Then add in a steady stream. Add lemon juice to taste, check seasoning and serve.

## Tip
For a lighter salad, halve the quantity of mayonnaise specified and replace half with the same quantity of Greek yoghurt.

# Citrus dressing

Serves 4

4 tablespoons olive oil
1 teaspoon lemon juice
finely grated zest of ½ lemon
1 garlic clove, peeled, chopped and mashed with a little salt
½ teaspoon wholegrain mustard

Whisk all the ingredients together, and check seasoning.

# Semi-sun-dried tomato pesto dressing

Thin Avoca semi-sun-dried tomato pesto with light olive oil and a drop or two of white wine vinegar. This works really well in dressings for pasta and couscous.

# Blue cheese dressing

Makes 400ml

100g blue cheese
200ml Greek-style yoghurt
200ml mayonnaise

Whisk with a hand blender until smooth.

# A basic dressing for pulses

1 garlic clove, peeled, chopped and mashed with a little salt
½ red chilli, finely chopped, or to taste
5 tablespoons extra virgin olive oil
juice of 1 lemon

Whisk the garlic and chilli into the oil, season with lemon juice, salt and pepper and dress still-hot pulses. Toss well so everything combines.

# Horseradish dressing

4 tablespoons olive oil
juice of ½ lemon
2 teaspoons grated fresh horseradish

Whisk all the ingredients together, adding more horseradish if you want a bigger kick. A few drops of Tabasco also works well.

This works particularly well with smoked fish and beef.

*Tasty - used cranberries I.L.O raisins*
*+ mint I.L.O*
*parsley + no celery + zatar I.L.O. ground coriander*

# Moroccan couscous

1 cup couscous
1 red and 1 green pepper
2 celery sticks, thinly sliced
2 teaspoons ground
coriander
1 teaspoon ground cumin
½ teaspoon chilli powder
½ cup raisins
125ml olive oil
4 tablespoons white wine
vinegar
1 bunch coriander
1 bunch flat-leaf parsley

*Moroccan cuisine is undoubtedly one of the great cuisines of the world, a heady mixture of spices and herbs, perfect for hot summer days. Lamb and chicken are the obvious partners to couscous but you could serve this salad with a yoghurt-based salad and some grilled vegetables to make an all-vegetable lunch without compare.*

Cook the couscous according to the instructions on the packet, then leave to cool. Deseed, core and dice the peppers into 5mm cubes. Add to the couscous along with the celery.

Combine the ground coriander, cumin, chilli powder, raisins and oil in a frying pan and warm gently over a moderate heat for 3 minutes. Stir in the vinegar and pour this mixture over the couscous. Finely chop the coriander and parsley – don't worry about including the stalks, they add crunch. Add the herbs to the couscous, season with salt and pepper and mix well.

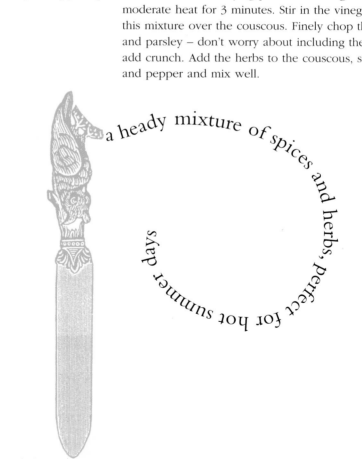

a heady mixture of spices and herbs, perfect for hot summer days

# Spiced lamb and couscous

2 leg of lamb steaks
2 tablespoons olive oil
juice of 1 lemon or 2 limes
1 teaspoon smoked paprika
1 teaspoon ground coriander
a pinch of ground cinnamon
a pinch of chilli flakes
a pinch of dried ginger
1 teaspoon ground cumin
a pinch of cayenne pepper

**Couscous**

1 small butternut squash,
peeled, seeded and cut into
4cm chunks
2 tablespoons olive oil
1 tablespoon flaked almonds
2 mugs couscous
4 scallions, trimmed and
finely chopped
1 chilli, finely chopped
1 heaped tablespoon sultanas
Bunch parsley finely
chopped
Bunch coriander, roughly
chopped

200ml yoghurt
1 garlic clove, peeled and
crushed with a little salt
½ cucumber, grated
bunch mint, chopped

*We've included this as a salad because it is possible to serve it warm and it can be presented on a platter at room temperature. This is an ideal dish for a barbecue, and if you have more than four guests, it's well worth considering a butterflied leg of lamb. Your butcher will do this for you. If you go this route you will need to increase the quantity of couscous and other ingredients.*

Combine the lamb with the next 9 ingredients. Season with salt and pepper and toss so everything is well combined. Set aside for a couple of hours or overnight in the fridge.

Preheat the oven to 180C/gas mark 4. Toss the butternut squash in 1 tablespoon of the olive oil, season with salt and pepper and roast for 30 minutes or until tender. Spread the almonds out on a shallow tray and put at the top of the oven until just coloured, about 4 minutes. Remove and set aside to cool.

Place the couscous in a bowl, pour over an equal quantity of boiling water and leave for 2 minutes. Fluff up with a fork and stir in the remaining tablespoon of olive oil. Combine the couscous with the scallions, chilli, sultanas and butternut squash. Season all with salt and pepper. Then add the parsley and coriander. Combine the yoghurt, garlic, cucumber and chopped mint and season with salt.

Season the lamb and grill or char-grill for 4-5 minutes on each side. Allow to rest and then slice. Serve the couscous with the lamb layered over the top and the yoghurt on the side.

# Swedish potato salad with potted salmon

700g new potatoes
4 tablespoons olive oil
1 teaspoon white wine vinegar
1 teaspoon wholegrain mustard
1 red onion, peeled and very finely diced
2 tablespoons chopped dill
1 tablespoon chopped chives
150ml soured cream or crème fraîche
2 tablespoons mayonnaise

**Potted salmon**

200g hot smoked salmon, flaked
3 tablespoons crème fraîche
1 bunch dill, chopped
juice of 1 lemon
1 teaspoon grated fresh horseradish

*This salad is very good with fish, particularly something that has come off the barbecue. Try sea bass or sea bream, barbecued so the skin becomes charred and crispy, leaving the flesh moist and succulent and ever so slightly smoky. Alternatively try with traditionally poached organic or wild salmon.*

For the salad, steam the potatoes (this helps to keep them dry inside) until cooked, about 15-20 minutes. Drain well and toss with the olive oil, vinegar and mustard.

Allow to cool and then combine with the other ingredients, tossing well. Season with salt and pepper.

For the salmon, combine all the ingredients in a bowl, mix with a wooden spoon and season to taste. (This will keep for several days in the fridge.)

In the cafes we serve the salmon in kilner jars. Or you might like to serve it in ramekins with the potato salad alongside.

## Variation

*You can use full-fat Greek-style yogurt as an alternative to the mayonnaise.*

## Tip

*You want your potato to be waxy rather than floury for a good salad. There are over 400 varieties of potato but only 40 are cultivated and even fewer are widely available. Varieties to look out for include: Jersey Royals (a king – or queen – among potatoes), Ulster Sceptre, Pentland Javelin, Désirée, Romano, Pink Fir Apple, Charlotte, La Ratte, Nicola, Roseval.*

*Look out for seasonal Irish potatoes. We find the ones from Wexford particularly good*

# Summer **fruit** salad

1.3kg/3lb ripe Galia melon
2 large oranges, zested,
peeled and segmented
2 large nectarines, skinned,
stoned and thinly sliced
1 punnet of strawberries,
hulled and cut in half
1 cucumber, halved
lengthways, deseeded
and sliced
3 tablespoons chopped
fresh mint
2 teaspoons icing sugar

Peel, deseed and dice the melon and mix with all the remaining ingredients in a large bowl, then taste and add more sugar if necessary. You can add some Pimms or Cointreau to this, which gives it a little more punch.

# Roast fennel and pepper with mangetout

*2 heads fennel, cored,*
*trimmed and sliced*
*4 tablespoons olive oil*
*1 red and 1 yellow pepper,*
*cored, seeded and cut into*
*thick strips*
*100g mangetout, cut into*
*thin strips*
*1 teaspoon sherry vinegar*
*2 garlic cloves, peeled and*
*finely chopped*
*1 bunch flat-leaf parsley,*
*finely chopped*

Preheat the oven to 200C/gas mark 6.

Toss the fennel in the olive oil. Season with salt and pepper, place in a roasting tin, and roast for 20-30 minutes until lightly charred. Add the peppers 20 minutes before the end. Remove both vegetables from the oven and allow to cool.

Blanch the mangetout in salted boiling water for 2 minutes, drain and refresh under cold water.

Toss the roasted vegetables and their juices with the mangetout, sherry vinegar, garlic and parsley. Pile on to a serving plate and drizzle over more oil if necessary.

# Char-grilled Mediterranean vegetables

1 aubergine, trimmed and
sliced
2 red peppers
2 yellow peppers
2 courgettes, trimmed and
sliced lengthways
2 red onions, trimmed,
peeled and sliced into discs
1 bunch asparagus
(about 250g)
olive oil
1 fennel bulb, trimmed and
sliced through the root
1 teaspoon picked thyme
leaves

*This salad is easy to do. It's really nothing more than char-grilled vegetables, yet the flavours are robust and rustic. It's a way of giving vegetables lots of attitude. Use a ridged griddle pan, well heated, or a barbecue. Drizzle the assembly with good quality olive oil and serve slightly warm.*

Toss the aubergine with a teaspoon of salt and leave in a colander to drain. Accepted wisdom was that this drew the bitterness out of the aubergine. However the main reason is to wilt the aubergine so it becomes softer. Leave for 20 minutes, rinse off thoroughly and pat dry.

Place the red and yellow peppers on a hot ridged griddle pan for 10-15 minutes, turning 2 or 3 times. These both need to be good and black all over. Remove, transfer to a bowl and cover with clingfilm.

Lightly brush the aubergine, courgette and red onion with olive oil and grill on the griddle pan. You want everything to be well marked but take care, it is easy to overdo the char bit.

Toss the asparagus in olive oil, season with salt and grill for 5 minutes, turning two or three times.

Blanch the fennel in boiling salted water for 5 minutes or until just tender. Drain and pat dry. Grill until well marked on both sides.

Skin and seed the peppers, tear into rough strips and transfer to a bowl with the juices. Add the other vegetables along with the thyme. Toss with more olive oil, season with salt and pepper and transfer to a platter.

## Variations
*Garnish with Parmesan shavings.*

*Serve as a light lunch along with a plate of charcuterie, black olives and good bread. Or alternatively with a plate of good anchovies dressed with olive oil, vinegar or lemon juice, and flat-leaf parsley.*

# Storecupboard

*Your salad needs the finest ingredients you can find. Let it down with less than the best and it will let you down too.*

*The following is a list of storecupboard items which enable you to ring the changes, add spice and variety:*

Extra virgin olive oil.

Small bottle walnut or
hazelnut oil
*(the snag is that once opened
it tends to go rancid
within a month or two).*

Small bottle pure sesame oil.

Good-quality sunflower
*(which is not the same as
vegetable)* oil.

Peanut oil.

Avocado oil and flax seed oil
*– particularly healthy.*

Aged balsamic vinegar – the
older the better.
*You use very little so a small
bottle really does last.*

Pomegranate syrup is a nice
alternative to balsamic.

Rice wine vinegar, *much less
acidic than white wine
vinegar and slightly sweet.*

Aged red wine vinegar.

Aged white wine vinegar.

Fish sauce (nam pla).

Sweet chilli sauce.

# Char-grilled chicken panzanella

4 skinned chicken breasts
2 tablespoons Avoca semi
sun-dried tomato pesto
1 ciabatta, torn into
4cm chunks
1 cucumber, trimmed,
seeded and cut into chunks
1 red onion, peeled and
finely chopped
150g tomatoes, cored and
roughly chopped
150g yellow cherry tomatoes,
halved
6 tablespoons olive oil
1 tablespoon red wine
vinegar
1 bunch basil, roughly
chopped

*This is traditionally served in Italy as a refreshing salad, and it makes use of leftover bread. It works wonders particularly when served cold straight from the fridge.*

Cut the chicken into strips and marinate in the sun-dried tomato pesto overnight, or at least for a few hours. Season with salt and pepper. Grill for 5 minutes on each side or until cooked.

Soak the bread in cold water until soft. Squeeze gently, and place in a bowl with all the other ingredients, except for the basil. Stir so everything is combined, season with salt and pepper and store, covered, in the fridge for a few hours.

Stir the chicken and basil into the salad just before serving

## Variations
*A red pepper, trimmed and cut into chunks, adds lots of crunch and an interesting flavour*

## Tip
*Soaking the bread in water is the traditional peasant route to panzanella. A modern take is to toast ciabatta, either cubed or in thin slices. This brings a different texture to the dish.*

# Avoca's three-bean

*400g can each of kidney beans, chickpeas and butterbeans, drained and well rinsed*
*4 spring onions, finely chopped*
*2 red and 2 yellow peppers, diced*
*1 small can of sweetcorn, drained and well rinsed*

*For the dressing:*
*1 tablespoon Dijon mustard*
*3 garlic cloves, peeled, chopped and mashed to a paste with a little salt, using the flat of a large knife*
*125ml extra virgin olive oil*
*Juice of 1 lemon*

*If you are catering for large numbers there is nothing to beat cooking your pulses from scratch, both for flavour and cost considerations. Yet canned pulses, particularly the European brands, are excellent and extremely easy both to store and use. You need to ensure they are well rinsed and left to drain.*

To make the dressing, combine the mustard and garlic in a large bowl, season with salt and pepper and then gradually whisk in the olive oil. Add the lemon juice to taste.
Stir the beans and vegetables into the dressing and mix well. Taste and adjust the seasoning.

# Chorizo, mixed bean and rocket

*4 tablespoons olive oil*
*250g cooking chorizo,*
*finely sliced*
*1 x 400g can butter beans,*
*well rinsed*
*1 x 400g can red kidney*
*beans, well rinsed*
*100g French beans,*
*blanched*
*and refreshed*
*1 shallot, peeled and finely*
*chopped*
*1 garlic clove, peeled,*
*chopped and mashed with*
*a little salt*
*2 tablespoons finely*
*chopped parsley*
*juice of 1 lemon*
*4 small handfuls rocket*
*leaves*
*4 dessertspoons Greek*
*yoghurt*

Heat the oil and when hot fry the chorizo slices for about two minutes each side. You want them to crisp up. Drain and set aside.

Add the beans to the hot oil along with the shallot, garlic and parsley, and stir-fry for 2 minutes. Return the chorizo slices to the pan. Season well with salt and pepper and add lemon juice to taste.

Allow to cool for 5 minutes, then toss with the rocket. Serve with plain yoghurt.

season well with salt

# Seared spiced beef with Asian greens and noodles

2 sirloin steaks (about 180g each), cut into thin strips
1 teaspoon five-spice powder
3 star anise, broken up
3 garlic cloves, peeled and roughly chopped
1 red chilli, finely sliced
3cm piece fresh root ginger, peeled and grated
1 tablespoon soy sauce
2 tablespoons vegetable oil
150g thin egg noodles
4 heads pak-choi, quartered lengthways
225g baby spinach
a bunch of scallions, finely sliced on the diagonal
150g mangetout, sliced lengthwise
4 tablespoons sesame oil
2 tablespoons rice wine vinegar
1 bunch coriander, roughly chopped
150g beansprouts
3 teaspoons sesame seeds, toasted

A tangy Asian-themed salad with lots of complex flavours. This is a meal in itself or it can be partnered with other dishes to form something of a feast.

Combine the beef with the five-spice powder, star anise, garlic, chilli, ginger and soy. Toss so everything is coated and set aside overnight in the fridge, or for at least a few hours.

Stir-fry the beef in a large wok or frying pan in the oil for 2-3 minutes, or until cooked. Remove and keep warm.

Cook the noodles in boiling unsalted water according to the instructions on the packet. Drain and refresh in cold water.

Mix the noodles and vegetables together. Add the beef and juices along with the sesame oil and rice wine vinegar.

Sprinkle with the chopped coriander, beansprouts and sesame seeds.

## Variation
Toasted cashew nuts are a delicious addition.

# Chickpea and spinach salad

2 400g tins chickpeas,
drained and rinsed
1 red onion, peeled and
finely chopped
2 tablespoons olive oil
1 teaspoon ground cumin
Half teaspoon paprika
Pinch saffron strands
400g spinach, stems removed
and roughly chopped
Juice and zest of 1 lemon
1 teaspoon tahini paste
1 garlic clove, peeled,
chopped and mashed with
a little salt
1 tablespoon finely chopped
parsley

Heat the olive oil over a low heat and gently cook the red onion for 10 minutes without colouring. Add the cumin, paprika and saffron. Cook for one minute and then add the spinach. Cook, stirring frequently, until wilted, about three minutes. And the zest from the lemon and half the juice.

Add the chickpeas to the spinach mixture, toss so everything is well coated and check seasoning. You may need a little water if it is looking dry.

Combine the tahini paste with the garlic and remaining lemon juice. Let it down with a a tablespoon or two of warm water and when the consistency of thick cream stir in the parsley. Drizzle over the chickpeas and serve.

# Chicken Caesar salad

For the Croutons:
2 large garlic cloves
3 tablespoons virgin olive oil
Half a baguette, cut into cubes

1 large egg yolk
3 tablespoons fresh lemon juice
1 medium garlic clove, crushed
4 flat good quality anchovies, mashed with a fork
1 teaspoon Dijon mustard
4 tablespoons olive oil
2 medium heads of romaine lettuce -- outer leaves removed
2 tablespoons grated Parmesan
200g cooked chicken, sliced

*A timeless classic, this salad continues to be very popular anytime we put it on the menu in the cafes. If the mayonnaise is a step too far at home try whisking three tablespoons of olive oil into a cup of Hellmann's.*

Smash the garlic with a large knife and place in a bowl with the olive oil and cubed bread. Toss well so everything is coated, decant on to a roasting tray and roast in a preheated oven, 200C/gas mark 6 for 10 minutes or until golden.

Break the egg yolk into a bowl and whisk in the lemon juice, garlic, anchovies and mustard. Add the oil, drop by drop at first and then in a slow stream so the dressing emulsifies.

Combine the lettuce, Parmesan and chicken in a bowl. Add the dressing and toss well so everything is coated. Scatter over the croutons and serve.

*Lemon*

*Why not just nuts & seeds*

*Salads are infinitely variable. Even small changes can transform a salad. Think nuts and seeds as well as spices and herbs. Here are a few to consider.*

The following bring more flavour if lightly toasted. The first three are Avoca favourites.

> Blanched hazelnuts
> Almonds
> Peanuts
> Pine nuts
> Pecan nuts
> Sesame seeds
> Sunflower seeds
> Linseeds
> Pumpkin seeds

To lightly toast, either add to a dry frying pan over a moderate heat or place under the grill. If you use the latter route keep a close eye, it takes very little time to toast nuts!

Walnuts are also good in salads, particular in autumn and winter, but they don't retain much crunch. Good with fruits.

*Spices work particularly
well with salads involving
pulses.*

Ground cumin and
ground coriander are
particularly good, but do
need to be dry roasted.

Ground chilli is very good
with couscous and pulses,
as are cinnamon and
ground ginger.

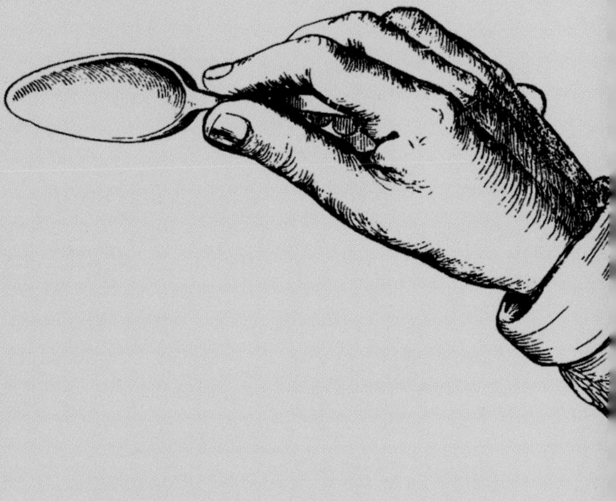

# Spices and pulses

# Tracy salad

3 potatoes peeled and diced
olive oil
balsamic vinegar
20 thin slices chorizo, cut on
the diagonal
4 handfuls rocket
8 semi sun-dried tomatoes
8 slices feta

*So called because it was created by Tracy McCormack, a friend of Simon Pratt's. The dish went on the menu in Suffolk Street in the early days and has proved so popular it has become a regular.*

Cook the potatoes in salted boiling water until tender and toss with salt and pepper 2 tablespoons of olive oil and dessertspoon of balsamic vinegar. Season with salt and pepper.

Preheat the oven to 180C/gas mark 4. Lay the chorizo slices out on a shallow baking tray and bake for 20 minutes in the oven.

Toss the potatoes in the baking tray so they absorb the chorizo flavour. Then combine with the rocket and add the chorizo along with any oil that has gathered in the roasting tray. Scatter over the sun-dried tomatoes and feta and serve.

# Coronation chicken

1 medium onion, peeled and
finely chopped
2 tablespoons olive oil
2 tablespoons mild curry
powder
30ml white wine
4 tablespoons mango
chutney
1 dessertspoon tomato purée
250ml mayonnaise
250ml Greek-style yoghurt
1 cooked chicken, shredded
2 heads little gem lettuce,
leaves separated
2 heads red chicory, leaves
separated
2 tablespoons finely chopped
herbs (chives, chervil,
tarragon, parsley)
12 seedless grapes, halved
1 tablespoon flaked almonds,
lightly toasted

*There is something gloriously retro about this dish. When we put it on the menu in the cafés, we really did wonder what the reaction would be. Unparalleled enthusiasm was the answer, some said like having an old friend back.*

Gently sauté the onion in the olive oil for 10 minutes without colouring. Add the curry powder and cook, stirring, for one minute. Add the white wine, and boil to reduce by half. Add the mango chutney and tomato purée. Cook over a low heat for 5-8 minutes, stirring occasionally. Push through a sieve, and allow to cool.

When cold, combine the curry sauce with the mayonnaise and yoghurt. Use enough sauce to coat the chicken generously.

Arrange the salad leaves on a platter, spoon the chicken over and garnish with the herbs, grapes and almonds.

## Tip
*The base sauce without the yoghurt and mayonnaise will keep for a week in the fridge in a sealed container.*

# Bacon, blue cheese and Baby spinach

1 tablespoon pine nuts
6 slices bacon, cut into lardons
4 tablespoons olive oil
2 garlic cloves, peeled and bashed
½ ciabatta loaf, cut into croûtons
4 handfuls baby spinach
1 teaspoon balsamic vinegar
4 tablespoons Cashel Blue (or similar soft blue cheese)

*For anyone not that keen on blue cheese, this salad is a perfect introduction. The power of the cheese almost slips away, making the salad elegant and creamy.*

Heat a dry frying pan and lightly colour the pine nuts. Transfer to a plate and allow to cool. Add the lardons to the pan, and continue to cook until just turning crisp. Transfer to kitchen paper using a slotted spoon. Add half the olive oil to the pan. Add the garlic and cook over a gentle heat until just starting to colour. Remove the garlic and discard.

Add the croûtons to the oil, toss and sauté until golden brown and crisp. Transfer to kitchen paper to drain.

Toss the spinach with the remaining olive oil, the balsamic vinegar and a seasoning of salt and pepper. Scatter over the lardons, croûtons and pine nuts. Crumble the Cashel blue on top and serve.

*Artisan cheeses to consider*
Cashel Blue, Crozier Blue, Beenleigh Blue, Colston Bassett, Dunsyre Blue.

. . . . . . . . . . . . . . . . . . . . . . . . . . . . . . . . . . . . . . . . . . . .

*Tip*
*If you want to serve a salad at a dinner party you may like to distribute it on individual plates, piling the main leaves up in the centre of the plate. You can then add more dressing (olive oil and drops of balsamic) around the edge of the plate, which gives it a good frame and adds colour and interest.*

# Marinated Asian chicken and noodles

4 chicken breasts
1 tablespoon sweet chilli
dressing
1 garlic clove, peeled and
finely chopped
1 red chilli, finely chopped
3cm piece fresh root ginger,
peeled and grated
1 tablespoon soy sauce
1 teaspoon fish sauce
(nam pla)
200g medium egg noodles
2 large handfuls beansprouts
1 red pepper, cored, seeded
and finely sliced
4 scallions, trimmed and
finely sliced
1 handful mangetout, finely
sliced lengthways
1 bunch coriander, roughly
chopped
2 tablespoons sesame oil
1 dessertspoon sesame seeds,
toasted

Combine the chicken with the dressing, garlic, chilli, ginger, soy sauce and fish sauce. Toss well and set aside.

Cook the noodles according to the instructions on the packet. Refresh under cold water, drain well and toss with the rest of the ingredients.

Preheat the grill, and grill the chicken for 6-7 minutes on each side or until cooked. Allow to rest for a few minutes, slice on the diagonal and serve on top of the noodle mixture. Season to taste.

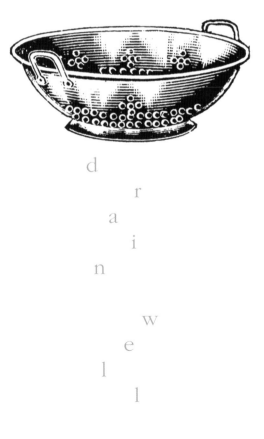

drain well

# Crab

2 medium-sized cooked
crabs
2 lemons, 1 juiced,
1 quartered
1/2 cucumber, finely diced
1 tablespoon mayonnaise
1 tablespoon finely chopped
chives
2 beef tomatoes, deseeded
and chopped
4 slices white or brown
bread
4 tablespoons olive oil
1 teaspoon white wine
vinegar
4 handfuls salad leaves

*This is a very dramatic salad, both to prepare and eat. It takes a bit of time to extract all the meat from a crab, but it's well worth it when you get to the end. Success with crab is all in the freshness.*

Smash the back edge of the crab firmly on a board. The shell can then be prised away from the body. Remove the dead man's fingers and discard. Drain off any liquid around the brown meat and scoop out with your finger into a bowl. Add any additional brown meat attached to the body to this bowl and mash lightly with a fork, seasoning with a little salt and lemon juice (the brown meat is quite strongly flavoured).

Remove the claws and legs from the bodies and set aside. Slice the bodies in half and pick out all the white meat – there is quite a lot in here. Crack the claws and pick the meat out and add to the the meat from the body. It is debatable if the legs are worth doing; a lot depends on how much time you have. Season the white meat with lemon juice and salt and pepper. Stir in the cucumber, mayonnaise, chives and tomato.

Toast or char-grill the bread. Spread with brown meat and then pile the white meat on top. Place on four plates.

Combine the olive oil with the vinegar, add salt and pepper, and toss with the salad leaves. Distribute between the plates, and serve with a lemon quarter.

## Tips

*We also serve this with brown bread in place of toast, and a salad of dressed baby leaves on the side.*

*You may have to order your crab in advance. A good fishmonger will sell them cooked and will prepare them for you, at a price.*

*To cook your own crab, place in well-salted lukewarm water. Bring to the boil slowly, add a 50ml of white wine vinegar and a few parsley stalks. Once boiling, simmer for 10 minutes or until the shell changes to red. Drain and allow to cool.*

*Tasty*

# Penne with rocket and semi-sun-dried tomato pesto

350g dried penne
2 tablespoons Avoca semi-sun-dried tomato pesto
olive oil
4 handfuls rocket leaves
100g semi-sun-dried tomatoes
2 tablespoons pitted black olives, chopped
1 teaspoon nigella seeds, toasted

To serve
freshly grated Parmesan

*Pasta salads generally make great picnic salads. They can be made up in advance, will weather the journey well and come up looking like they have just been made.*

Cook the pasta in plenty of salted boiling water until just tender, then drain.

Toss with the pesto, adding a little olive oil and cooking water if it seems too thick.

Add the remaining ingredients, and serve with the Parmesan sprinkled over the top.

## Variations
*Asparagus*
*Char-grilled courgettes or aubergines*
*Roasted red and yellow peppers*
*Crispy pancetta, crumbled in at the end*

*Other cold pasta salad combinations to consider:*
*Feta, black olive, caper and fresh oregano*
*Tuna, sun-dried tomatoes and green olives*
*Fresh cherry tomatoes with ricotta cheese and basil*
*Lemon (zest and juice), mint and ricotta cheese*

*Large shells or similar shapes tossed in Avoca semi-sun-dried tomato pesto and extra virgin olive oil with baby mozzarella balls, slow-roasted cherry tomatoes, torn basil leaves, oregano, semi-sun-dried tomatoes and kalamata olives*

# Classic Niçoise

4 large tomatoes
1 cucumber
1 red pepper, deseeded and
cut into thin strips
8 radishes
2 scallions
a generous handful of
French beans
1 garlic clove
4 tablespoons olive oil
1 scant teaspoon white
wine vinegar
4 hard-boiled eggs, peeled
and quartered
1 can good-quality tuna,
drained
4 white anchovy fillets
(available from
delicatessens)
1 tablespoon pitted black
olives
2 lemons, halved

*All the sunshine of the Mediterranean rolled up into one salad, with a glass of chilled rosé to accompany, maybe.*

Core, seed and quarter the tomatoes, and season with salt. Seed the cucumber then slice and season with salt. Char-grill the pepper until black, transfer to a bowl and cover with clingfilm (see page 9). When cool enough to handle, core, seed and tear into strips. Thinly slice the radishes and scallions. Blanch the beans in well-salted boiling water, drain and refresh under cold water.

Peel and slice the garlic and then mash with a little salt to form a purée in a salad bowl. Whisk the olive oil into this with the white wine vinegar.

Add all the prepared vegetable ingredients to the bowl with the dressing, and toss well. Arrange the eggs, tuna, anchovies and olives on top, and serve with a lemon half for each person.

· · · · · · · · · · · · · · · · · · · · · · · · · · · · · · · · · · · · · · · · · · · · · · · · · · · · · · · · · · · ·

## Eggs

*We use free-range eggs. Organic are also good. A small producer is even better. An egg needs to be viscous, the yolk a deep yellow and as fresh as possible.*

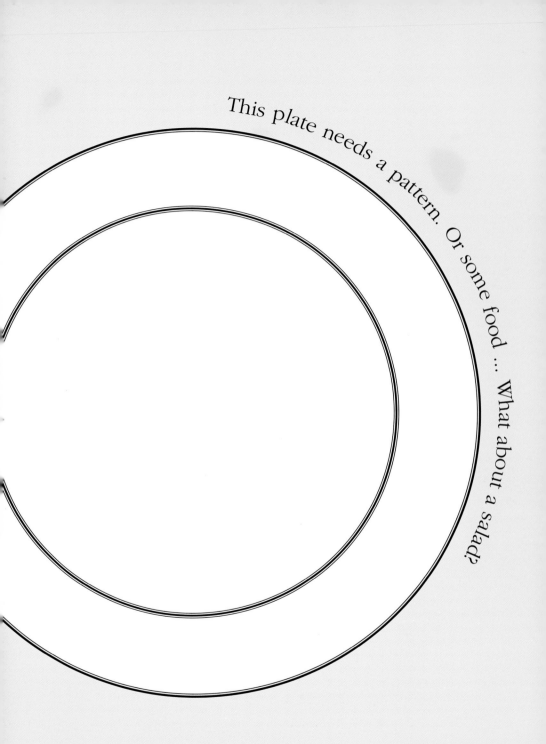

This plate needs a pattern. Or some food ... What about a salad?

Hmmm ... what will I cook?

Food for thought:

..............................................................................................

..............................................................................................

..............................................................................................

..............................................................................................

..............................................................................................

# Endive, Cashel Blue and pear with toasted hazelnuts

*2 red or white heads*
*chicory*
*juice of 1 lemon*
*4 tablespoons olive oil*
*Tabasco sauce*
*2 pears*
*2 dessertspoons shelled*
*hazelnuts*
*100g Cashel Blue cheese*

Trim the endive, cut in half lengthways and then slice lengthways as thinly as possible. Turn on their sides and slice again so you end up with long thin strips. Toss in a bowl with lemon juice, salt and pepper and olive oil to taste. Add a few drops of Tabasco.

Peel, core and slice the pears. They will need more lemon juice to prevent browning. Toast the hazelnuts under the grill until they just colour. You need to shake them a little to ensure they are evenly coloured. Remove, allow to cool and roughly chop.

Pile the endive in the centre of four plates. Lean the pear slices up against the tangle of endive, crumble and scatter over the Cashel Blue, and finish with a shower of the hazelnuts.

*Endive*

# Roast cherry tomatoes

250g red cherry tomatoes
250g yellow cherry tomatoes
7 tablespoons extra virgin
olive oil
1 teaspoon icing sugar
1 head garlic, cloves
separated and lightly
crushed
1 teaspoon picked
thyme leaves

*This is something of a multiple-use salad. Serve by itself with bread or with grilled meat or fish.*

Preheat the oven to 120C/gas mark ½.

Combine the tomatoes in a roasting tray, pour over 4 tablespoons of the olive oil and dust with the icing sugar. Season with salt and pepper, tuck the garlic in and roast in the oven for 45 minutes to an hour, or until some of the tomatoes start to burst.

Transfer to a platter and scatter over the thyme leaves. The garlic should be soft and melting and can be squeezed out of its skin. Drizzle with the remaining extra virgin olive oil.

## Variations

*You can add torn mozzarella to the cooling tomatoes. Or black or green olives, pitted are best. You could use basil or oregano in place of the thyme.*

*You could also add roasted fennel, which needs to be quartered, seasoned, drizzled with olive oil and roasted at 180C/gas mark 4 for 40 minutes or until tender.*

# A simple green salad
## of baby leaves

*4 generous handfuls salad leaves*
*4 tablespoons olive oil*
*1 scant teaspoon balsamic vinegar*

*A green salad to accompany grilled meat or fish? Or a green salad beefed up with other ingredients to make it a meal in a bowl? This salad is one of the most versatile.*

Combine all the ingredients in a large bowl, season with salt and pepper and toss just before serving.

### Variations

*There are endless possibilities. Chief among them are herbs: in summer the likes of tarragon, chives and chervil; in winter something more robust, perhaps parsley, coriander, even celery leaves. Edible flowers, like nasturtiums or marigolds, add both colour and flavour. And then there are the more spicy leaves, like sorrel, mizuna, red mustard and watercress.*

*Very thinly sliced smoked duck or chicken breast.*
*Char-grilled nectarines (see page 67).*
*Quartered figs.*
*Slices of Parma ham with or without shaved Parmesan and toasted pine nuts.*

# A bigger salad

## To the leaves above add:

*3 large ripe tomatoes, cut into eighths*
*100g canned chickpeas, drained and rinsed*
*2 carrots, scrubbed and cut into batons*
*100g canned white asparagus tips, drained and chopped*
*30g pine nuts, toasted in a dry frying pan*
*30g Parma ham, dry-fried until crisp*
*50g Parmesan, shaved*
*3 scallions, finely chopped*

# Duck, lentil and frisée

2 duck confit legs, shredded
1 x 400g can Puy lentils,
well rinsed
1 head frisée lettuce, washed
1 tablespoon walnut oil
3 tablespoons light olive oil
1 teaspoon pomegranate
syrup
lemon juice
a handful of shelled
fresh walnuts
seeds from 1 pomegranate

*A classic French salad given something of a modern twist with the pomegranate seeds. If pomegranates are not in season try pine nuts which are very different but rather delicious.*

Combine the duck, lentils and frisée in a bowl. Season with salt and pepper and toss well.

Combine the oils, syrup, a seasoning of salt and pepper and lemon juice to taste. Toss the salad mixture in the dressing and scatter over the walnuts and pomegranate seeds.

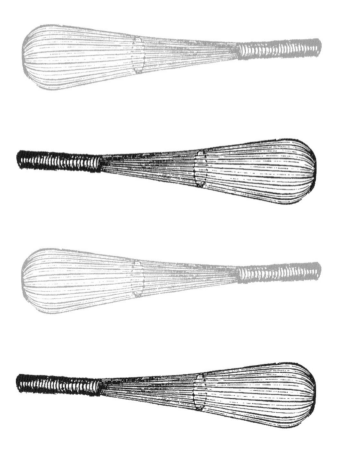

# Baby spinach, pancetta, avocado and Swiss chard leaves

*8 slices pancetta*
*1 tablespoon pine nuts*
*2 handfuls baby spinach*
*2 handfuls baby Swiss chard leaves*
*4 tablespoons olive oil*
*1 teaspoon balsamic vinegar*
*2 ripe avocados, peeled, stoned and diced*
*2 tablespoons semi-sun-dried tomatoes*
*10 red and 10 yellow cherry tomatoes, halved*

Grill the pancetta until well coloured and crisp. Set aside on kitchen paper. Toast the pine nuts in a dry frying pan over a moderate heat until lightly coloured. Transfer to a plate to cool.

Combine the spinach and chard leaves, season with salt and pepper and toss with the olive oil and balsamic vinegar in a bowl. Scatter over the pine nuts, avocado and all the tomatoes. Top with the crispy pancetta and serve.

Tip *Toss the avocado lightly in lemon or lime juice to stop discoloration*

# Puy lentils, rocket
## and feta

100g Puy lentils
1 red chilli
4 garlic cloves, 2 unpeeled, 2
peeled and finely chopped
4 tablespoons olive oil
1 tablespoon finely chopped
shallot
2 tablespoons chopped
parsley
1 teaspoon balsamic vinegar
4 handfuls rocket leaves
4 tablespoons semi-sun-dried
tomatoes
150g feta cheese, crumbled
½ teaspoon picked thyme
leaves

*You can also use green or brown lentils in this salad. Puy lentils seem to deliver more flavour, colour and texture, but all lentils are popular with customers.*

Place the lentils in a saucepan along with the chilli and unpeeled garlic, and cover with water by 2cm. Bring to the boil, removing any scum from the surface, then simmer slowly for 20 minutes or until cooked. Remove and drain discarding the garlic. Toss with the olive oil, chopped garlic, shallot, parsley and balsamic vinegar and allow to cool.

When the lentils are cool, combine with the rocket, semi-sun-dried tomatoes and toss well. Check the seasoning. Add the feta on top and sprinkle over the thyme.

## Variations
*You can lightly toast walnuts and add them just before serving.*
*Duck confit goes really well with this, either hot as a piece, or flaked into the lentils.*

Draw your favourite fruit inside the frame

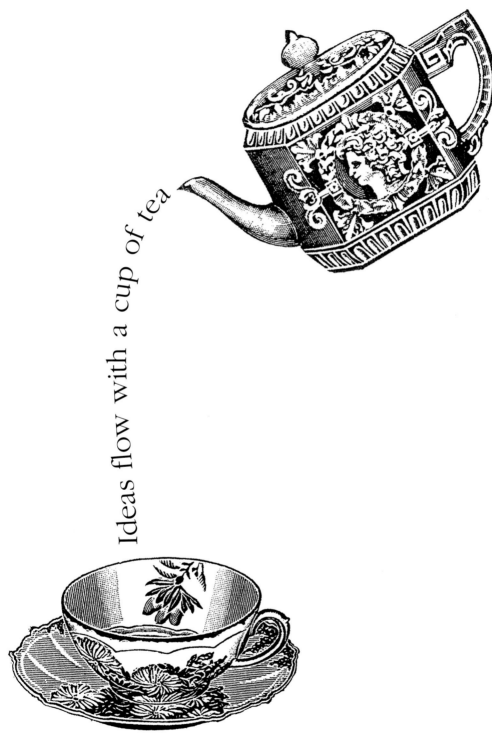

Ideas flow with a cup of tea

# Carrot with roasted sesame seeds

*1 dessertspoon sesame seeds*
*4 coarsely grated carrots*
*Avoca French dressing*
*(see page 22)*

*Simple and full of colour, this is a combination that works so well it seems as classic as Caesar or niçoise. The carrot's pedigree is important; choose organic if possible and nothing too old. Crunch and a good colour are essential. Lacklustre specimens need not apply. As far as quantities are concerned, this salad should be made to taste. As a guide, use about a tablespoon of sesame seeds to 5 large carrots. You could use other seeds such as poppy, pumpkin or linseeds, or substitute pine nuts.*

Roast the sesame seeds in a dry frying pan over a moderate heat until lightly coloured. Alow to cool, add them to the grated carrot and toss with 3 tablespoons of French dressing. Check the seasoning and serve.

# Smoked tuna, rocket
## and cannellini beans

*100g dried cannellini beans,
soaked in cold water
overnight
1 red chilli
4 garlic cloves, 2 unpeeled,
2 peeled and crushed with
a little salt
1 bunch parsley, picked
4 tablespoons olive oil
juice of 1 lemon
1 red onion, peeled and very
finely diced
2 tablespoons semi-sun-dried
tomatoes
4 handfuls rocket leaves
250g smoked tuna,
gently broken up*

*This is a favourite salad in our Suffolk Street café where we serve it with crusty bread. An ideal one-course lunch. We use tuna from Woodcock Smokery.*

Place the cannellini beans, chilli and unpeeled garlic in a saucepan along with the stalks from the parsley, and cover with water by 2cm. Bring to the boil, removing any scum from the surface, and simmer slowly for an hour, or until cooked. Remove and drain.

Toss the still-hot beans with the olive oil, lemon juice and crushed garlic. Allow to cool.

Add the finely diced red onion, semi-sun-dried tomatoes and mix with the rocket and parsley. Scatter over the smoked tuna and serve.

## Variation
*The salad is also very good with smoked salmon.*

# Barbecued nectarines

8 nectarines
1 tablespoon caster sugar
juice of 1 lemon

*Serve these as a salad to accompany barbecued meats or with mascarpone or crème fraîche as a pudding. Or with ice-cream, vanilla is particularly good.*

Preheat the char-grill or barbecue.

Cut the nectarines in half and scatter over the sugar. Char-grill or barbecue for a couple of minutes.

Transfer to a bowl, and season with lemon juice to taste.

## Variations

*You can skewer the fruit with lavender or rosemary stalks, both of which add flavour and look very good.*

*You can combine the sugar with a few tablespoons of rose water for a different flavour.*

*Pour a little Vin Santo or sweet dessert wine into the centre of each nectarine before serving.*

# Broccoli, cherry tomato, feta and hazelnut

110g hazelnuts
400g broccoli florets
(bite-sized)
110g feta cheese, cut into
bite-sized cubes
225g cherry tomatoes, halved
200ml Avoca French dressing
(see page 22)

Toast the hazelnuts in a hot oven (see page 54), then tip them into a tea towel and rub off the skins. Allow to cool, then put the hazelnuts in a bowl with the broccoli and cherry tomatoes. Gently toss with the dressing and season with pepper. Salt may not be required, since the feta is usually salty enough. Top with the feta.

wine water

juice smoothies

milk tea

beer cider

# Char-grilled
## asparagus stalks

*2 bunches asparagus*
*4 tablespoons extra virgin*
*olive oil*
*Maldon sea salt*
*1 teaspoon balsamic vinegar*
*1 tablespoon Parmesan*
*shavings*

*Asparagus needs only the most simple of treatments to give of its best. Eat the stalks by themselves, or partner with some cheese and charcuterie for a snack or first course, or grilled meat or fish for a main.*

Preheat a ridged cast-iron griddle pan. Toss the asparagus in the the olive oil, season with salt and chargrill for 5 to 8 minutes, turning two or three times.

Transfer to a plate, and season again with salt and pepper. Toss with the balsamic vinegar and scatter over the Parmesan shavings.

. . . . . . . . . . . . . . . . . . . . . . . . . . . . . . . . . . . . . . . . . . . . . . . . . . . . . . . . .

*Variation*
*Add dried red chilli flakes just as the asparagus comes off the grill.*

or                    Pre-heat 400°

Put Asparagus on grill pan
Drizzle olive oil + salt
+ pepper
Sprinkle over mozerella +
parmesan
Bake 10 mins
+
Extra 5 mins in grill

X

# Potato and mint

900g small new potatoes
2 tablespoons Avoca French
dressing
(see page 22)
6 tablespoons mayonnaise
2 tablespoons plain yoghurt
A large bunch of mint,
chopped

*As classic as they come. Buy the best potatoes you can and leave the rest to nature. And don't skimp on the salt. This is not the time to be worrying about over-indulgence; reserve that for the next time you are tempted by a packet of crisps.*

Place the potatoes in a pan of salted water and bring to the boil. Simmer for about 15 minutes or until tender, then drain and place in a bowl. Mix with the French dressing and leave to cool. Mix the mayonnaise, yoghurt and mint together and toss with the potatoes. Season with salt and pepper and serve.

**Editor** Hugo Arnold
**Photography** Georgia Glynn Smith
**Art Direction and Design** Lucy Gowans
**Production** Tim Chester

Text © 2007 Hugo Arnold
Photography © Georgia Glynn Smith

First published in 2007 by Avoca Ltd,
Kilmacanogue, Co Wicklow

Printed and bound in Hong Kong by South Sea
International Press

Cataloguing-in-publication datea:
A catalogue record for this book is available
from the British Library
ISBN 978-0-9538152-4-1